Mount Erebus looms over
McMurdo Station, Antarctica.

"Where the telescope ends, the microscope begins. Which of the two has the grander view?"

—Victor Hugo, *Les Misérables*

LIFE
on Earth—and Beyond
An Astrobiologist's Quest

Pamela S. Turner

For Lauren, Ryan, and Justin
—P. S. T.

Published by Charlesbridge
85 Main Street
Watertown, MA 02472
(617) 926-0329
www.charlesbridge.com

Library of Congress Cataloging-in-Publication Data
Turner, Pamela S.
    Life on earth—and beyond / Pamela S. Turner.
        p. cm.
    ISBN 978-1-58089-133-2 (reinforced for library use)
    ISBN 978-1-58089-134-9 (softcover)
1. Exobiology—Juvenile literature. 2. Space biology—Juvenile literature. 3. Life on
other planets—Juvenile literature. 4. McKay, Christopher P.—Juvenile literature. I. Title.
QH327.T87 2008
571.0919—dc22   2007001475

Printed in Singapore
(hc) 10 9 8 7 6 5 4 3 2
(sc) 10 9 8 7 6 5 4 3 2 1

Display type and text type set in Mister Earl and Stempel Garamond
Color separations by Chroma Graphics, Singapore
Printed and bound by Imago
Production supervision by Brian G. Walker
Designed by Diane M. Earley

Table of Contents

The Hubble Space Telescope is able to
photograph distant galaxies, such as the
barred spiral galaxy NGC 1672.

Are We Alone?

Biology is the study of life on Earth, but astrobiology is the study of life in the universe. Astrobiologists seek to answer the question: does life exist beyond Earth?

We haven't discovered any aliens yet. However, astrobiologists are looking carefully at planets such as Mars, moons such as Europa, and distant solar systems for signs of life. Astrobiologists like Dr. Chris McKay of the National Aeronautics and Space Administration (NASA) also study extreme environments on Earth to better understand how life might survive the extreme environments on other worlds. Chris's research takes him to places such as Antarctica, the Atacama Desert in Chile, Russia's Siberia, and Africa's Sahara Desert. What types of creatures live in these harsh environments? How do they survive?

Could similar life be waiting beyond Earth?

Lack of rainfall, less than 4 inches (10 centimeters) of snow per year, and temperatures of minus 29°F (minus 34°C) make the Dry Valleys a frozen desert.

1

Between a Rock and a Cold Place

The Dry Valleys, Antarctica

The Antarctic Dry Valleys (the dark patches in this satellite photo) are the largest ice-free areas in Antarctica.

Can life survive in a very cold, dry place?

At the very bottom of the globe, in a land of ice and snow, there are great curving valleys of bare earth: Antarctica's Dry Valleys. It's a harsh place. In April, the beginning of the Antarctic winter, the sun goes down and doesn't come up again until September. For months the Dry Valleys are locked in frozen darkness. There isn't a single scraggly weed or tiny insect. The Dry Valleys are almost as lonely as outer space.

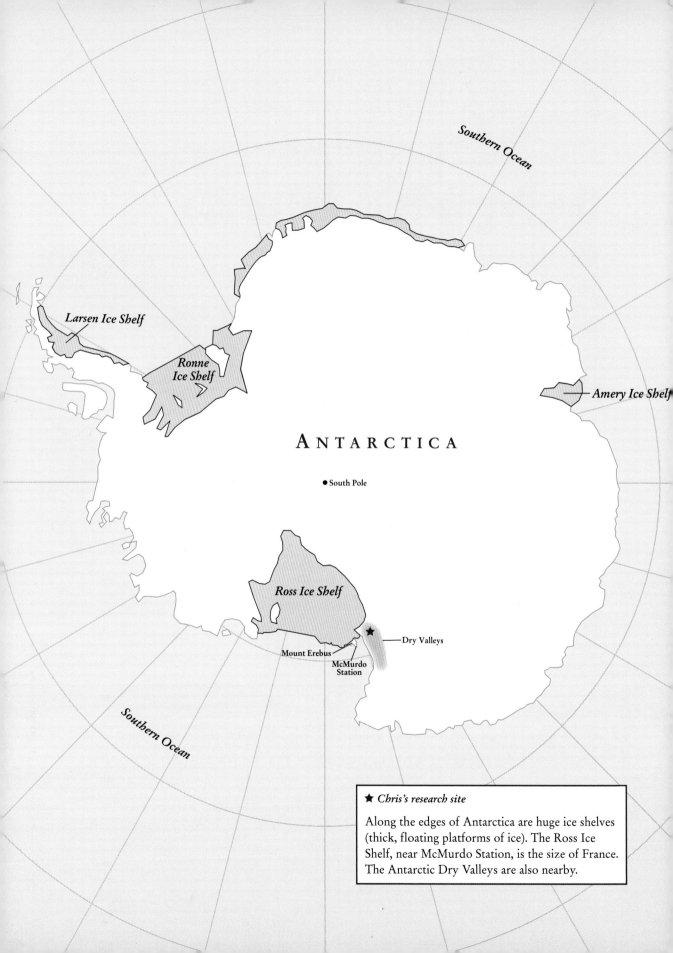

Southern Ocean

Larsen Ice Shelf

Ronne Ice Shelf

Amery Ice Shelf

ANTARCTICA

● South Pole

Ross Ice Shelf

Mount Erebus

McMurdo Station

★ Dry Valleys

Southern Ocean

★ *Chris's research site*

Along the edges of Antarctica are huge ice shelves (thick, floating platforms of ice). The Ross Ice Shelf, near McMurdo Station, is the size of France. The Antarctic Dry Valleys are also nearby.

Yet the Dry Valleys fascinate astrobiologists like Chris McKay. "The Dry Valleys are like Mars," explains Chris. "Both are cold and dry. It hardly ever snows in the Dry Valleys, and when it does, the air is so cold that very little snow ever melts. Mars is even colder and drier."

Chris set off to visit the Dry Valleys in January 2005, during the Antarctic summer. Just getting to such a remote spot was an adventure.

Journey to the Bottom of the Earth

To reach the Dry Valleys, Chris flew from San Francisco, California, to New Zealand. In New Zealand he boarded an Air Force cargo plane to McMurdo Station in Antarctica. The cargo plane had no reclining seats or meal service. No windows either. "It was eight hours of being cramped and cold, and so noisy you had to wear earplugs," Chris later recalled.

Chris and seven other scientists took many boxes of equipment to Antarctica. They didn't have to bring everything, however. The scientists had special cold-weather clothing and camping gear from the National

Chris's team boards a cargo plane for the flight from New Zealand to Antarctica.

Science Foundation, an agency that coordinates American research in Antarctica. They didn't have to pack food either. Chris and the other scientists went shopping at McMurdo Station's "supermarket": a big metal hut full of groceries.

After stuffing two helicopters with camping gear, equipment, food, and water, the scientists flew to the Dry Valleys. They landed atop a giant lump of sandstone called Battleship Promontory. It would be their home for the next two weeks.

Helicopters carried the scientists, their supplies, and their equipment 100 miles (160 kilometers) from McMurdo Station to the Dry Valleys.

Chris and his colleagues camped atop Battleship Promontory.

Scientists have found seal mummies in the Dry Valleys.
Some of them are thousands of years old.

Little Green Men

Early on his first morning in the Dry Valleys, six-foot-six-inch Chris wormed his way out of his extra-long sleeping bag. There was plenty of light outside. The sun is up twenty-four hours a day during the Antarctic summer. However, the sun's rays didn't give off much warmth. Even during the summer the Dry Valleys were as cold as Montana in winter.

Chris dressed quickly and made his way through the scientists' tent camp. The chilly wind cut like a razor, even through down-filled clothing.

The camp was a little "tent city." There was a science tent, a kitchen tent, a toilet tent, and the "suburbs" (the sleeping tents). Solar panels powered the kitchen tent, fondly nicknamed Café Battleship. Chris treated his companions to pancakes with canned cherries on top. Cleaning up was easy. The scientists just wiped everything with paper towels and let the dishes freeze. Nothing rotted or spoiled in the cold, dry air.

Chris serves pancakes inside Café Battleship.

This is the camp on Battleship Promontory. At the end of the trip, helicopters flew out every piece of trash and human waste.

This is the view from Chris's tent. In 2005 there was more snow than usual.

Chris has been making these camping trips to Antarctica for twenty-five years. He knows there are creatures hidden in the Dry Valleys that can survive some of the world's worst weather. Their secret? They live *inside* rock.

"Solid" rock isn't always solid. Many rocks are honeycombed with little spaces, or pores, that seem like huge caverns to super-small creatures called microbes. Microbes (also called microorganisms) are the tiniest of all living things. They are so small that they can't be seen without a microscope.

After breakfast Chris headed to the nearby sandstone cliffs. He examined the sandstone carefully. Chris spotted little blotches on the rock. A colony of microbes was living in pores just under the surface. With a hammer and chisel he carefully chipped off a chunk of rock to take back to his lab at NASA. On previous visits Chris had drilled tiny holes into the sandstone and attached sensors. The sensors measured the light and moisture inside the rocks year-round. Chris's sensors showed that the microbes hidden in the rocks survived on tidbits of summer sunlight and a few drops of snowmelt.

Looking carefully, Chris also spied a wet spot on the rock. "When that happens there are microbes cheering, 'Yeah! Wet snow!'" Chris later explained. "They are living in little rock greenhouses. They 'wake up' for a few days in the summer, when the sun is shining and a little moisture seeps down through the pores in the rock. They grow a little and then go back to sleep for the rest of the year."

Chris chipped off another rock sample. Just under the rock's surface was a thin green line—a minute "forest" of microbes (cyanobacteria and fungi). These microbes were real survivors. "If life exists on Mars, it might look something like that," Chris later explained. "Those little green critters are the best Martians we have. And everyone knows Martians are little and green!"

Snowmelt reaches the microbes that are hidden inside the rock.

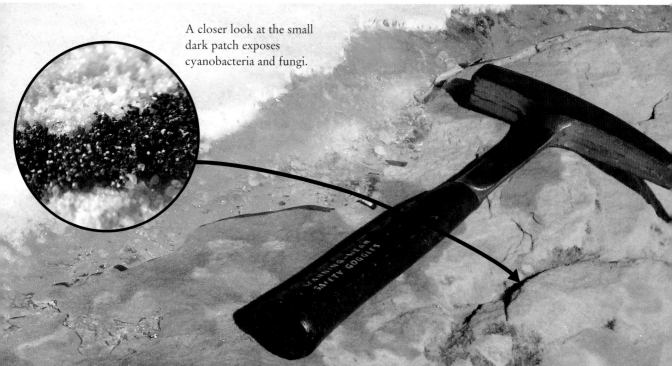

A closer look at the small dark patch exposes cyanobacteria and fungi.

A shelter of rock or dirt would be very important for any Martian life. The atmosphere on Mars is too thin to block dangerous radiation from the sun. If any life exists on Mars, it would need to be shielded from solar radiation by rock or soil. But microbes hiding inside rocks or underground aren't easy to find. So Chris used the Dry Valleys as a testing ground for microbe-detection machines.

What Is Life?

You'd think the answer is easy. Living things eat (take in energy) and give off waste, right? But a car "eats" gasoline and gives off heat and exhaust gases. A car isn't alive.

Let's add the ability to reproduce. A car can't make baby cars.

That doesn't work either. A fire eats wood and oxygen and gives off heat, carbon dioxide, and smoke. It can reproduce, too. A single spark can grow into a whole new fire.

Let's add the ability to evolve. Fire can't do this. Fire is fire. But all species of living things—from bacteria to bean plants to bears—evolve. They adapt over time in response to changes in their environment. So now we have it: a living thing eats, gives off waste, reproduces, and evolves.

Sorry, but there is one major glitch: viruses. Viruses are very small, very simple microbes. They cause many human diseases, including AIDS and the common cold. Viruses take in energy, give off waste, and evolve. Flu viruses evolve so quickly that scientists must develop new flu vaccines every year to fight the latest version of the virus.

But viruses can't reproduce by themselves. A virus must invade the cell of a living thing (such as a bacterium, plant, or animal) and hijack the cell's machinery to make more viruses.

So is a virus just a fancy bit of chemistry? Or is it possible for something to be half-alive?

Scientists are still arguing over these questions. There's no easy answer. That's life!

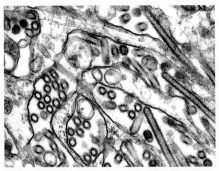

The gold circles and rods are the deadly H5N1 "bird flu" virus.

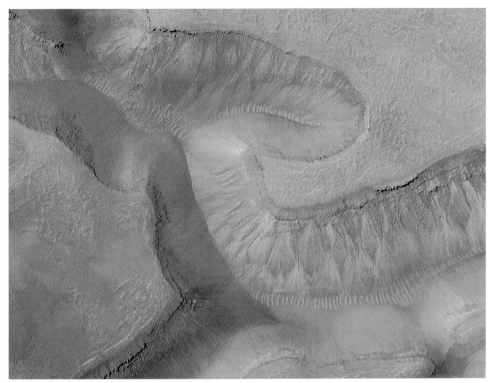

These are valleys on Mars. The average temperature on Mars is minus 80°F (minus 60°C), but the temperature can reach 70°F (20°C) during the Martian summer.

Machines for Mars and Beyond

The team brought a gas chromatograph, a spectrometer, and four types of ultraviolet (UV) lasers to test in the Dry Valleys. Each machine used a different technique for sensing hidden microbes. The gas chromatograph sensed gases given off by microbes. The spectrometer looked for the kind of light absorbed by microbes. The UV laser sensed the "glow" given off by microbes when the UV laser shone on them.

At least that's what was *supposed* to happen. But the gas chromatograph didn't work at all, despite hours of tinkering. Of the six machines Chris and the other scientists brought to Antarctica, only two, the spectrometer and one UV laser, were good at finding microbes. Even recording test results was difficult. The ink froze in Chris's pen!

Chris was pleased that two machines worked. Science is all about testing new things and ideas. Sometimes things work out, and sometimes they don't.

A spectrometer or UV laser may travel on a future NASA mission. The machines may land on a planet that—like the Dry Valleys—seems too cold and too dry for life. Yet "little green men" might surprise us.

Chris can't wait to find out. He's been wondering what's out there ever since he found a dusty old telescope and pointed it into the night sky.

Kevin Hand, Robert Carlson, and Henry Sun test a spectrometer on rock containing hidden life.

Chris phones home via satellite. The blue squares provide solar
power for the scientists' equipment.

Bug-eyed Guys with Flying Saucers

Scientists think that aliens on other planets are most likely to be microbes, not bug-eyed guys with flying saucers. Why is this?

Microbial life is the simplest kind. Complex animals take much longer to evolve. As a result, microbial life should be far more common in the universe than complex life.

Simple, hardy microbes are also able to live in environments that are too harsh for complex life. That means many more possible homes are out there for alien microbes than for bug-eyed guys with flying saucers.

2

Evolution of a Scientist

The Mars Underground

Chris grew up and attended school in Florida.

In August 1975 *Viking 1* left Earth to look for life on Mars.

How did Chris become an astrobiologist?

While growing up in Florida, Chris didn't pay much attention to NASA, Mars, or ideas about little green men in outer space. He spent his time playing in nearby orange groves with his sister and seven brothers. He did have an early interest in science, though. "I got a chemistry set one Christmas, and I read a lot of science books," Chris remembers.

In high school Chris took all the science courses offered. He liked physics the best. "In physics there were just a few basic concepts you could apply over and over," said Chris. "But I hated marine biology. There were too many facts you had to memorize, like the name of this or that squid."

Chris also liked tinkering with machines. Once he took his motorcycle completely apart. "I unscrewed every single bolt, took apart every gasket, and put it all back together again," said Chris.

As a college student at Florida Atlantic University, Chris majored in physics. One day he found a dusty telescope in a laboratory closet. Chris fixed it up and gazed at the stars and planets. He read books about making telescopes and built his own. "I was amazed you could take sand and two pieces of glass and make all the lenses you need for a telescope," recalled Chris.

Chris and Penny Boston were both founding members of The Mars Underground, a student group interested in sending astronauts to Mars. Penny now studies rock-eating microbes that live in deep, dark caves.

Chris was so hooked on space science that he decided to study astrophysics (the physics of objects in outer space) in graduate school. It was good timing. A new kind of space science—astrobiology—was just getting started.

What's Out There?

People had wondered about alien life for a long time. In the late 1800s Percival Lowell, a wealthy amateur astronomer, claimed Mars was crisscrossed with a network of canals built by intelligent Martians. It seemed possible. After all, Mars, like Earth, was the right distance from the sun for life. A planet close to the sun would be too hot, and one far away would be too cold.

As it turned out, canals and intelligent aliens on Mars were the result of wishful thinking and fuzzy telescopic images. The unmanned spacecraft *Mariner 4* flew by Mars in 1965 and sent back the first photos of Mars from space. Mars was cold, dry, and lonely. It made the Sahara Desert look cozy.

Images from *Mariner 4* were captured as numbers printed on strips of paper. Too anxious to wait for the official processed image, employees hand colored the numbers on the strips like a paint-by-numbers picture.

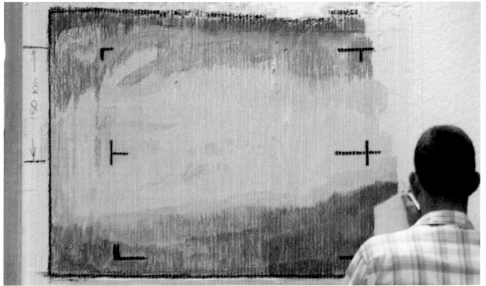

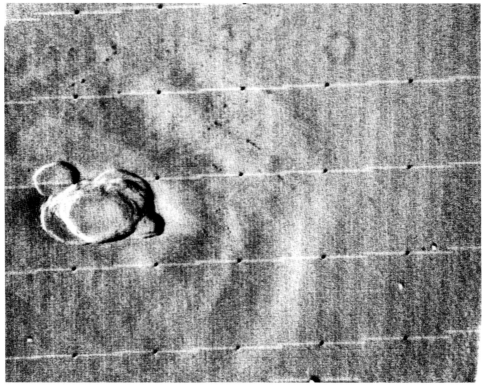

This photo of craters and ridges on Mars was taken by *Mariner 9*.

In 1971 *Mariner 9* orbited Mars. Mars was dry and dusty, but the more detailed *Mariner 9* photos showed canyons, ridges, and valleys that looked as if they had been carved by water. Scientists wondered if the Red Planet had once been warmer and wetter. Could life have evolved during that time?

The unmanned *Viking 1* and *Viking 2* spacecrafts landed on Mars in 1976, just as Chris was beginning graduate school in astrophysics at the University of Colorado at Boulder. The *Viking* landers (space vehicles designed to land on a planet or moon) carried three simple experiments that tested the Martian soil for signs of life. After checking the results, scientists decided that Mars appeared dead.

When Chris heard about the *Viking* missions, he was fascinated. "Here was a planet that had the potential for life, but apparently no life,"

Io

Jupiter

Europa

Ganymede

Callisto

A composite of photos
taken by *Voyager 1* in 1979.

This is one of the first
photos of the Martian
surface taken by *Viking 2*.

said Chris. "The lights were on, but nobody was home. Why not? I wanted to figure out what life needs to exist. That's how I got interested in astrobiology."

New Missions to Mars

Chris met other students at the University of Colorado who shared his interest in Mars. They thought NASA should send astronauts to Mars to explore the planet firsthand. But NASA's manned space explorations seemed to be ending with the *Apollo* Moon missions. Going to Mars would be much harder than going to the Moon, of course. It was a far longer, more difficult trip. But the students thought it could be done. They thought it *should* be done.

Chris (left) first visited Antarctica with Imre Friedman (right).

Some microbes thrive in super-hot and super-acidic hot springs.

Chris wrote a note to a professor asking permission to hold a conference on sending astronauts to Mars. "He sent the note back with a big red NO across it," recalled Chris. "We did it anyway."

They called their conference "The Case for Mars." It was a huge hit. "We were stunned so many people came," said Chris. "We had real scientists come, people from NASA." A reporter called Chris and his friends the Mars Underground.

After the Mars conference, Chris spent the summer at NASA's Ames Research Center in Mountain View, California. There he met Imre Friedman. Imre studied microbes that survived in harsh places by living inside or under rocks. He invited Chris to join him on a trip to the Antarctic Dry Valleys. Imre knew microbes were there, inside the rocks, but he didn't know what they needed to survive. That would be Chris's job. As the "gadget guy," Chris built sensors to monitor the temperature, light, and moisture inside the rocks year-round. He created his sensors from parts he bought at a RadioShack store in Colorado.

Going to the Dry Valleys was an incredible experience for the young scientist. "It was my first trip outside the United States," Chris said, remembering it fondly. "Antarctica is still my favorite place."

Chris's trip to Antarctica also introduced him to microbes in extreme environments. These microbes—some of the weirdest creatures on Earth—were giving astrobiologists new ideas about the kind of life that might exist *beyond* Earth.

New Worlds on Earth and Beyond

Every time scientists looked carefully at an extreme environment, they seemed to find microbial life. There were microbes in hot springs

Scientist T. C. Onstott and his colleagues recently discovered microbes living in pockets of hot salt water more than a mile (over 2 kilometers) underground. The microbes have been completely isolated from the surface for at least three million years and survive by eating minerals in the rock.

Astronaut Pete Conrad of *Apollo 12* stands next to *Surveyor 3*.

acidic enough to dissolve steel nails. There were microbes in super-salty lakes, inside radioactive waste dumps, and miles underground. Some Earth bacteria even survived two years on the airless Moon. The bacteria accidentally stowed away inside a camera sent to the Moon on *Surveyor 3*. Two years later the camera was brought back to Earth by *Apollo 12* astronauts, and the little space hitchhikers were revived in a lab.

Is Anybody Home?

Microbes in extreme environments on Earth have taught scientists that life can exist in some very unusual places. These are the top spots in the search for life beyond Earth:

MARS: UNDERWORLD?

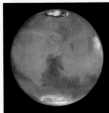

Mars is called the Red Planet because of its rust-colored dirt and rocks.

MARS is cold and dry. Its atmosphere is so thin that surface life would be exposed to damaging solar radiation. Billions of years ago, though, Mars probably had lakes and oceans. Could life have evolved on Mars during that time? Could it still be there, hiding inside rocks or underground near pockets of liquid water? If Martian life evolved and then died out, did it leave behind any traces?

EUROPA: WATERWORLD?

Europa is a moon of Jupiter.

SCIENTISTS think Europa, a moon of Jupiter, is covered by a layer of ice one-half mile to six miles (one to ten kilometers) thick. There are cracks in Europa's icy shell—hints of an ocean below. Scientists think that the tugging of Jupiter's gravity on Europa's underwater crust may cause undersea volcanoes. Volcanoes, in turn, may fuel deep-sea hydrothermal (hot water) vents. Communities of animals live around deep-sea vents on Earth. Could there be vent life on Europa?

Want to know the exact number of extrasolar planets discovered to date? Check out NASA's PlanetQuest website: **http://planetquest.jpl.nasa.gov/index.cfm**

VENUS: CLOUDWORLD?

Venus is the planet closest to Earth.

FOR many years scientists thought super-hot Venus couldn't support life. But billions of years ago, Venus was cooler and wetter. Some scientists now think microbial life might have evolved on the surface and adapted to living in its thick clouds, which have Earthlike temperatures and pressures. Although no Earth microbes live their entire lives in the air, Venus's clouds are thicker and more stable than Earth's. Could life be floating above Venus?

ENCELADUS: GEYSERWORLD?

Enceladus is a small moon of Saturn.

YOU'VE probably never heard of Enceladus, a small moon circling Saturn. Astrobiologists didn't pay much attention either until NASA's unmanned *Cassini* probe flew by in 2006. *Cassini* discovered a huge geyser on Enceladus that spits water vapor and dust into space. Scientists think the geyser is fed by pockets of liquid water just under the moon's icy surface. Where there's liquid water, there's hope for life. Could little Enceladus produce a big surprise?

EXTRASOLAR PLANETS: A WORLD OF WORLDS?

Could NGC 300, a nearby galaxy, harbor Earth-like planets?

AN extrasolar planet is a planet that orbits a sun other than our own. Astronomers have now found hundreds of extrasolar planets. Most are giant gas planets, which are the easiest to find because they are so big. But in 2007 a smaller planet called Gliese 581c was detected. The planet probably has Earthlike temperatures. But does it have an atmosphere? Does it have liquid water? Nobody knows—at least, not yet.

Bacteria survived a trip to the moon and
back in *Surveyor 3*'s camera.

Scientists also found microbes living in the black depths of the sea. In 1976 scientists aboard the deep-diving submarine *Alvin* discovered microbes eating chemicals that were spewing out of super-hot vents on the ocean floor. The microbes, in turn, were eaten by a community of other animals such as clams and shrimp. It was the first-known community of life on Earth that wasn't directly dependent on sunlight for energy.

Just a few years later, the unmanned spacecraft *Voyager 1* flew past Europa, one of Jupiter's moons. *Voyager's* cameras showed that cracked

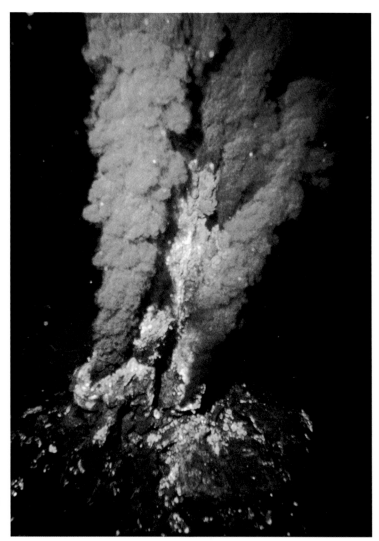

This is an undersea hydrothermal (hot water) vent.

ice covered Europa. It looked just like sea ice on Earth. Beneath Europa's icy crust, a planetwide ocean could exist. If Earth's oceans harbored life around deep-sea vents, maybe it could happen on Europa, too.

Scientists realized that microbes on Earth were tougher and more adaptable than they had ever dreamed. Perhaps microbes could survive on Mars, Europa, or other places in the universe.

These ideas energized the new science of astrobiology. Chris finished his PhD and joined NASA as a research scientist. By studying extreme environments on our own planet, he hoped to figure out the limits of life beyond Earth. His background in physics would help him understand the physical environment (such as light levels, temperature, and moisture). His work with microbes in Antarctica would help him understand the biology of extreme survivors.

Chris knew that the most important ingredient for life, anywhere on Earth, seemed to be liquid water. But was water really necessary for life? To find out, Chris needed to locate and study the driest places on Earth.

In 1996 several NASA scientists claimed that this four-and-a-half-billion-year-old meteorite from Mars held fossils of Martian microbes. Most scientists (including Chris) now think the evidence of life in the meteorite is faint, at best. Yet the meteorite made people think more about the possibility of life on Mars.

3

Is Life Liquid?

Atacama Desert, Chile

Since there was nobody on Mars to take the rover's picture, Hollywood-style special effects were used to create this image of *Spirit* on Mars.

Can life exist in a hot, dry place?

In January 2004 two robotic rovers landed on Mars. *Spirit* rolled through Gusev Crater. On the opposite side of the planet, *Opportunity* puttered around a dusty plain called the Meridiani Planum. NASA sent the rovers to Mars to find out if the planet once had liquid water—enough liquid water for life to exist. In searching for aliens, NASA's motto is Follow the Water.

Caribbean Sea

GUYANA

SURINAME

Caracas

VENEZUELA

Georgetown

Paramaribo

Cayenne

Bogotá

COLOMBIA

FRENCH
GUIANA

★Quito

ECUADOR

BRAZIL

PERU

SOUTH AMERICA

★Lima

BOLIVIA

La Paz

Brasília ★

Sucre

Pacific Ocean

PARAGUAY

CHILE

Antofagasta ★

Asunción

ARGENTINA

Montevideo

Santiago ★

Buenos Aires ★

URUGUAY

Atlantic Ocean

★ Chris's research site

  Atacama Desert

The Atacama research station is near the town
of Antofagasta, Chile. The Atacama desert
stretches for 600 miles (970 kilometers) along
Chile's western coast.

As *Spirit* and *Opportunity* were humming around Mars, forty million miles (sixty-four million kilometers) away Chris and his NASA colleagues were exploring the Atacama Desert in South America. They weren't "following the water." They were looking for spots with as little water as possible.

Very Little Rain on the Plain

To get to the Atacama, Chris and several other scientists and students spent a day flying from San Francisco to Antofagasta, Chile. From

This is an aerial view of the scientists' camp.

The scientists slept in tents at their research station in the Atacama.

Antofagasta they drove two hours through the desert to a research station. (It took *Spirit* and *Opportunity* seven months to get from Earth to Mars!)

The research station was just a desert shack that housed a kitchen and laboratory. Water was brought in by truck. The scientists pitched their tents along a line of scrubby trees left over from an agricultural experiment. The trees were the only bits of green for miles around.

Soon after arriving Chris checked his weather sensors. It had rained a few weeks before. "It was the biggest rain since 1994—about a fifth of an inch," recalled Chris. "For the Atacama, that's a flood!"

When Chris first visited the Atacama in 1994, he set up sensors to measure rainfall. For two years his sensors didn't record a single drop of rain. Chris thought they were broken, but they weren't. The lack of water was good news. Chris had found the driest desert in the world. The Atacama is even drier than Antarctica's Dry Valleys.

"There are lots of places where people say it doesn't rain, like the Gobi Desert in Mongolia, or the Australian outback," explained Chris. "But the Atacama is truly the driest place we've found." In fact, if the sky over the Atacama were reddish instead of blue, the super-dry desert would look a lot like super-dry Mars.

The rocky landscapes of the Atacama (left) and Mars (right) look quite similar.

Chris examines a rock in the Atacama.

Looking for Life in the Atacama

Chris and his colleagues tested the Atacama's soil and rocks for evidence of life. They tried some of the same soil experiments used by the *Viking* spacecrafts when they visited Mars in 1976. "If *Viking* had landed in certain areas of the Atacama, its tests would have said Earth is a dead planet," said Chris.

Chris tried other experiments. He brought rocks from other deserts and put them in the Atacama. On the underside of the rocks were microbes adapted to living in very dry places. The Atacama killed even those hardy microbes.

The Atacama isn't entirely dead, though. Some of the Atacama soil Chris collected did have live microbes. "We wondered how they survived," said Chris. "Did they grow in the Atacama? Or were they blown in by the wind, and we found them just before they died?"

A small pump hanging from the green balloon sucks in air, which will be checked for microbial life.

To find out if the microbes fell from the sky, Chris needed to take samples of the air over the Atacama. If the microbes were blown into the Atacama by the wind, the air would have about the same amount of microbes no matter where in the Atacama Chris took a sample. The conditions on the ground below—less dry or super-dry—shouldn't affect the number of microbes up in the air.

Chris brought along a helium balloon. The balloon was hard to handle in the desert wind. It bounced around like a crazed ping-pong ball. "It went every direction but up!" recalled Chris.

A small pump hung from the balloon. Once the bucking balloon was in the air, Chris turned the pump on using a remote-control device. The pump sucked a bit of air into a sealed dish. The balloon was pulled down, the dish removed, and a new one inserted. Later all the sealed dishes were brought to the lab and checked for microbial life.

Chris holds the air-sampling balloon to keep it from flying off.

While Chris was in the Atacama, NASA rovers were scrambling around Mars. At left is a ridge in the Atacama; at right is a photo of a Martian ridge taken by the *Spirit* rover.

Chris found that the air over the less dry areas of the Atacama had microbes, while the air over the super-dry spots had no microbes at all. The balloon tests suggested that the Atacama microbes weren't visitors carried by the wind. Chris thinks that in the less-dry parts of the Atacama, microbes grow in the soil. The dirt is then kicked up into the air by the wind. That would explain why the amount of microbes in the air was the same as the amount of microbes in the dirt below.

One thing is clear, however: in the very driest parts of the Atacama, nothing can survive. There does seem to be a limit to life on Earth. "At first I hoped I could find a microbe in the Atacama that was somehow adapted to life without liquid water," said Chris, "but it seems that where there is no liquid water, there is no life."

There may be no liquid water on Mars now, yet the Mars rovers *Spirit* and *Opportunity* proved that once upon a time Mars *did* have liquid water—lots of it. *Spirit* found rock that had once been soaked in water. *Opportunity* discovered wavy bands of rocks formed by a

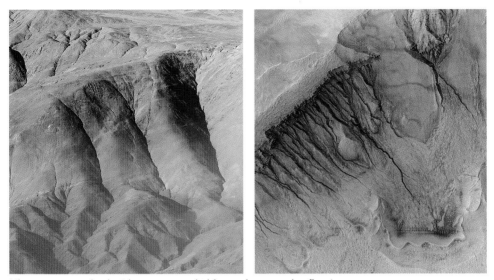

The grooves on both ridges were probably cut long ago by flowing water. (The Atacama is on the left. Mars is on the right.)

Water, the Host with the Most

Unless lost in a desert, we take water for granted. After all, it falls from the sky, and we flush it down the drain. But liquid water is a remarkable substance. Water is the essential molecule in the chemistry of life on Earth.

Imagine that life is a big party, and the most important elements of life (carbon, oxygen, nitrogen, hydrogen, and phosphorus) are the guests. Water is the host. Water is the one who gathers all the guests together and introduces them to each other. Water makes sure everyone's comfy—neither too hot nor too cold. Without water, the chemicals necessary for life couldn't find each other, mix with each other, and react with each other. Life would never happen.

In the party of life, water is the life of the party!

From space you can see that Earth is a big, water-covered sphere.

Chris and a student set up equipment on a hillside in the Atacama.

long-lost sea. Scientists think Mars's surface had water for hundreds of millions of years. That's enough time for life to have evolved. So where might we find traces of ancient Martians?

Chris thinks that evidence of early Martian life may be in a natural underground freezer on Mars. A natural underground freezer just like the one in Siberia.

4

Rip Van Microbe

Siberia, Northern Russia

In the summer Siberia becomes a land of lakes.

Can life survive in permafrost?

In many ways Siberia is the exact opposite of Mars. Siberia is full of life and water. There are vast herds of caribou and lakes and rivers splashing with fish. Yet Mars and Siberia have something in common: permafrost, a frozen mix of soil and ice.

Scientists have long wondered what lies beneath all that red dirt on Mars. Some scientists thought that Mars, like Siberia, had a great deal of frozen water locked under the surface. In 2002 the orbiting *Mars Odyssey*

Arctic Ocean

Kolyma River

RUSSIA

A S I A

Berin

Sea of Okhotsk

★ Ulaanbaatar

MONGOLIA

North Pacific Ocean

NORTH
KOREA

Beijing ★

Pyongyang ★   JAPAN

★ Seoul

CHINA

SOUTH
KOREA

★ Tokyo

INDIA

NEPAL

BHUTAN

★ Thimphu

Dhaka ★

MYANMAR

LAOS

TAIWAN

BANGLADESH

★ Hanoi   Hong Kong

Rangoon   Vientiane

*South
China Sea*

THAILAND

Bangkok

VIETNAM

Philippine Sea

★ Manila

★ Phnom Penh

CAMBODIA

PHILIPPINES

BRUNEI

Kuala Lumpur ★   MALAYSIA

SINGAPORE

★ Jakarta   INDONESIA

PAPUA
NEW GUINEA

Port Moresby ★

★ *Chris's research site*

The Kolyma River in Siberia (northeastern
Russia) flows north into the Arctic Ocean.
The river is ice free for only a few months
of the year.

spacecraft aimed a special gamma-ray instrument at Mars and discovered huge bands of underground permafrost on the Red Planet. Dusty Mars didn't lose all its water after all. Some water is still there, hiding underground. Could Martian life be frozen inside?

An artist's conception of the *Mars Odyssey* spacecraft that discovered the bands of permafrost on Mars.

The Russian research camp was near the Kolyma River.

In 1989, long before *Mars Odyssey*, Chris was thinking about Siberia. He knew that Siberia had deep, ancient permafrost and that there might be permafrost on Mars. Siberia could be a good stand-in for Mars. He hoped to find frozen life in Siberia—and he wanted to wake it up.

Scientists flew to camp in an old Russian army helicopter.

The mosquitoes were so abundant that the researchers sometimes wore bee hats.

Breakfast, Anyone?

Chris pulled on tall rubber boots and squelched through the muck to the drilling site. It was almost midnight, but a good time to start work. The clouds of mosquitoes weren't quite so thick, and there was plenty of light. Siberia is so far north that during the summer the sun never sets.

Chris and two other scientists, one Russian and one American, worked the drill. It was slow going. Every few feet they pulled up the drill and took it apart. The drill was hollow like a straw. Inside was a tube of permafrost that the drill had sliced from the frozen ground. The scientists carefully took the permafrost out of the drill core. It looked like a very untasty salami made of gray mud. The permafrost sample was put in a container, labeled, and stored in a natural Siberian freezer—that is, a hole in the ground.

Chris's Russian and American colleagues prepare the drilling equipment.

Chris drilled all night long. Finally, tired and hungry, he walked back to the research station for breakfast. The Russian scientists were gathered around a table in the kitchen tent, slicing up a bloody slab. "Breakfast," one of the Russians said cheerfully. "Moose liver!"

Suddenly, Chris wasn't so hungry anymore.

Imprisoned in Ice

The Russian and American scientists set up a lab at the research station to study the permafrost samples. They carefully cut the samples open and examined thin slices of permafrost under a microscope. The scientists used magnetic signatures in the permafrost to figure out its age. (Earth's magnetic field changes over time, and these changes, recorded in magnetic minerals, can be used to date soil.) They found that the oldest permafrost had been stored in nature's deep freeze for three and a half million years.

Soil frozen into permafrost, like most soil on Earth, is full of bacteria. The scientists put food that soil bacteria like to eat in a lab dish. They added some of the frozen bacteria from the ancient permafrost and let the bacteria thaw. Incredibly, after being frozen for three and a half million years, some of the bacteria revived. They began eating and reproducing. After all, they had to make up for thirty-five thousand centuries of lost time!

It is amazing to think that those Siberian bacteria were woken up by a species—modern humans—that didn't exist three and a half million years ago. When those Siberian bacteria went into their long, cold sleep, our ancestors were still halfway between ape and human.

A Russian scientist prepares a permafrost sample.

Who's Who?

If you've seen pictures of microbes, you've probably noticed that they look a lot alike. Many of them look like gummy worms. But with gummy worms at least you know the red is probably cherry flavored and the green is probably lime.

Not being able to tell microbes apart has been a problem for scientists. Scientists love to name and sort things. Unfortunately, scientists have always had a difficult time naming and sorting microbes. Many microbes look alike on the outside, even when their chemistry (what is happening on the inside) is wildly different. So microbiologists (scientists who study microbes) grow microbes in the lab and try to figure out what they are by what they eat. It is a little like trying to tell the difference between two animals by offering them a dinner of steak and salad and then watching what they choose. That might work for a lion and a rabbit, but it does not work as well for a lion and a tiger.

Microbiologists are now using genetics to help classify microbes. A genetic code is a chemical recipe that allows an organism—man, mouse, or microbe—to reproduce. When scientists compare the genetic code of different microbes, they can figure out which microbe is which. They can also tell how closely different kinds of microbes are related. The genetic code is a shortcut that helps scientists figure out who's who.

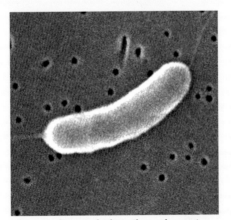 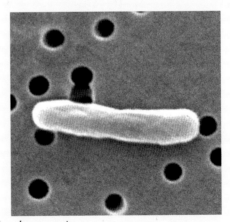

These two bacteria look similar under a microscope, but they are quite different. The bacterium on the left lives in warm seawater. The bacterium on the right lives in the digestive tracts of humans and other mammals.

Only the top few feet of Siberian soil thaws during the summer.
The deeper soil, called permafrost, stays frozen.

Martian Deep Freeze

Chris thinks that if life on Mars evolved in a warmer, wetter time, then it might be preserved in underground Martian permafrost. Unfortunately, if we found any frozen Martians, they couldn't be revived like the Siberian microbes were. That's because Mars's wet period ended three billion years ago. Martian rocks and soil give off a tiny bit of radiation, and after three billion years that radiation would have harmed any frozen Martians. They would be too damaged to revive. Yet finding an actual Martian would still be amazing. It could also tell us something important about life on Earth.

"If we found fossils in Martian rocks, that would be great," said Chris. "But a fossil is just a 'stamp' on a rock. A fossil can't tell us if Martian life is related to Earth life. To do that, we'd need to look at genes. If we could find frozen Martian life, even if it were very, very old, we

During Chris's trip, the Russian scientists found a 200-year-old corpse in the frozen ground.

could look at its genetic code and compare it to the genetic code of life on Earth."

A genetic code is carried in every cell of every living thing. It is the "recipe" for making that organism. If Martian life and Earth life shared the same genetic code, that would suggest we had a common origin. Microbial life might have begun on one planet and then traveled to another. The microbes' "spaceship" would most likely be a rock. Scientists think that microbes inside a rock could survive being knocked off one planet by an asteroid impact. The rock might then fall to another planet as a meteorite. If Earth life really began on Mars, that would make all of us Martians!

Chris hopes that if we find Martian life, it *isn't* like Earth life. "Truly alien life would be a lot more interesting," said Chris. "It would mean there are lots of ways for life to get going in the universe. Who knows what we'll find?"

This area on Mars looks like dirt-covered pack ice. There may
be a thick layer of ice under the red dust, or perhaps the ice
evaporated long ago, leaving only the pattern behind.

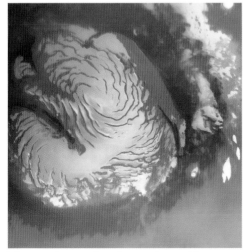

The Martian north polar cap is roughly 680
miles (1,094 kilometers) across. The white
areas are ice.

Inside this 20-mile-wide (32-kilometer-wide)
Mars crater is a coating of ice.

Itsy Bitsy Family Tree

The tree of life (at least life as we know it here on Earth) has three major branches, called domains. Two domains are made up entirely of microbes. That's fitting because microbes are in many ways the dominant form of Earth life. Microbes exist in far greater numbers and come in a far greater variety than bigger creatures such as animals and plants. They are also crucial in making the Earth habitable for all other life-forms. Microbes help plants grow, break down waste, and release oxygen into the air. There are even microbes in our stomachs that help us digest our food.

So where do scientists put viruses? Viruses don't get a twig on the tree of life, since scientists can't decide if they are alive or dead.

All life on Earth falls into one of three domains:

DOMAIN BACTERIA

Bacteria are very small, single-celled microbes. Their cells have no nucleus (a separate place inside the cell that holds genetic material). Cyanobacteria are a type of bacteria that use sunlight to grow.

DOMAIN ARCHAEA

Many microbes found in extreme environments, such as scalding hot springs, are archaea. Scientists used to think archaea were a kind of bacteria because archaea, like bacteria, are single-celled creatures without a nucleus. However, when scientists compared the genetic codes of bacteria and archaea, they were shocked. Bacteria and archaea may look similar, but genetically they are very, very different. People and mushrooms are more alike, genetically, than bacteria and archaea. Because of this, scientists gave archaea their own domain.

DOMAIN EUCARYA

This is the third major branch on the tree of life. Eucarya can be single-celled microbes like amoeba and certain algae and fungi. Eucarya can also be multicellular creatures such as animals and plants. However, all eucarya, whether as tiny as an amoeba or as big as a whale, have one thing in common: each cell has a nucleus that holds the genetic material.

5

Mother of All Deserts

The Sahara, Northern Africa

The Sahara is the biggest desert in the world.

How different are microbes in similar extreme environments?

Life on Earth has adapted to all sorts of extreme environments in all sorts of amazing ways. Chris hopes to study as many of these extreme environments as possible.

Although Chris had studied many deserts around the world—like the Atacama in South America and the "frozen desert" of the Antarctic

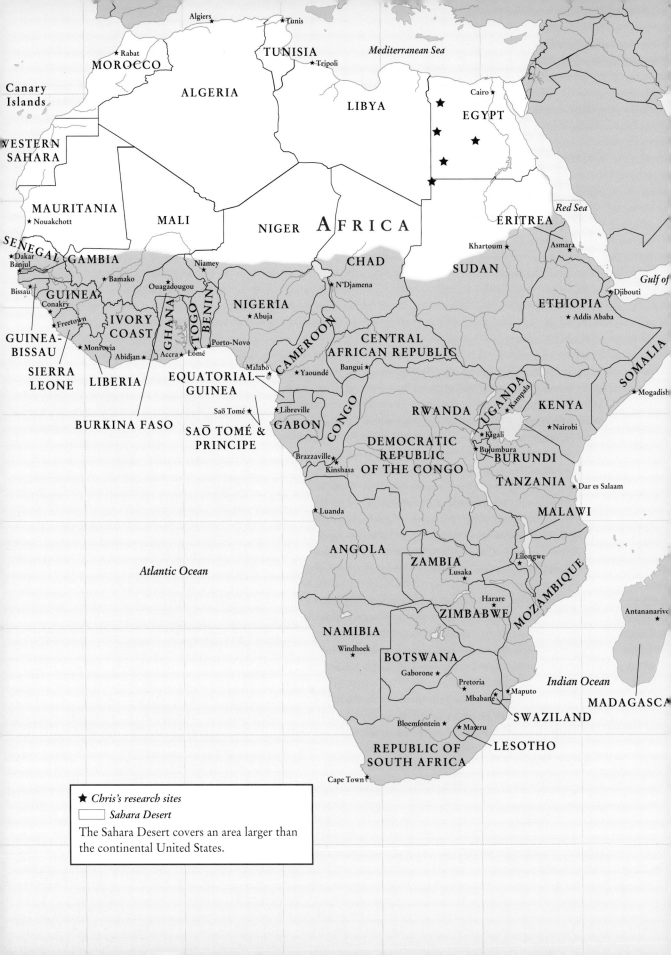

Dry Valleys—he had never visited the Sahara. So Chris, along with Margarita Marinova, a graduate student in geological and planetary science at California Institute of Technology, traveled to North Africa in November 2005 to find the dry core of the world's biggest desert. Usually Chris's trip companions are other scientists. But for this adventure, science teamed up with art.

Ancient Sahara, Ancient Mars

Chris and his companions drove for days across the sands of North Africa's Sahara. There were no roads. The Egyptian drivers used landmarks and a Global Positioning System (GPS) device to keep them from getting lost. Just in case, the Land Rovers carried lots of extra supplies.

During several weeks of travel in the Sahara, Chris's group never saw another person.

A truck rusts away in the harsh desert.

Migrating birds fly
across the Sahara.
Some don't survive.

"There are two essential liquids in the Sahara: water and gasoline," said Chris. "If you run out of either, it can cost you your life."

Chris and Margarita wanted to visit remote parts of the Sahara to learn what sort of microbes live there and how the Saharan microbes are like—or unlike—microbes in other deserts. Neither Chris nor Margarita had ever been to the Sahara, however, so they joined a trip led by an experienced guide. The trip was run by people interested in the ancient rock art of the Sahara.

Art in the Sahara? Why would anybody paint or sculpt in the middle of a vast desert?

Ten thousand years ago the Sahara wasn't a desert at all. There were forests and fields of grass. Giraffes, crocodiles, elephants, and ostriches lived in the Sahara. People also lived there. They drew and carved

Giraffes, cattle, and men with bows and arrows fill the walls of an ancient rock shelter.

pictures of themselves on rocks all over the Sahara. They drew the Sahara's animals, too.

Then the weather changed. The water holes, grasses, and trees dried up. The animals died or moved further south, where the land was still green. So did the people.

In some ways the Sahara is like Mars. Mars is much different today than it was in the past. It once had an atmosphere that acted like a blanket, protecting Mars from the chill of space. The Martian atmosphere kept the planet warm enough for liquid water to form into lakes and oceans.

Billions of years ago Mars may have looked like this.

This is an artist's conception of a time when Mars was warmer and wetter—a place where life could evolve.

Mars had one fatal flaw: its size. The smaller a planet is, the weaker its gravity. Mars is only half the size of Earth, so Mars's gravity wasn't strong enough to hold its atmosphere. Very slowly, over hundreds of millions of years, Mars's atmosphere leaked out into space. Mars grew colder. Most of its water evaporated or froze into permafrost.

If Martian life evolved and died out, Chris hoped it left behind fossils or traces, just as the vanished people of the Sahara left behind their paintings and carvings.

Earth's Greatest Disaster

Two billion years ago, the Earth was horribly polluted. A deadly poison swept the planet. Almost all life on Earth died out. The killer's name? Oxygen.

A billion years before this disaster, there was hardly any oxygen in our air. Earth's atmosphere was mostly carbon dioxide, like the atmosphere of Mars today. There were no birds, or bugs, or flowers on Earth. The carbon dioxide atmosphere could not block deadly ultraviolet (UV) radiation from the sun. Nothing could live on land. The only living things were primitive microbes in the oceans. Ocean microbes survived because water blocks UV radiation.

Some of the microbes living in the ocean were a type of cyanobacteria. These cyanobacteria evolved the nifty trick of using sunlight and water to get energy. The process is called photosynthesis. Oxygen is the waste left over from photosynthesis.

Earth's cyanobacteria were as happy as tiny little globs could be. They chugged along for hundreds of millions of years, gobbling up sunlight and water and spewing out waste oxygen.

Bit by bit, eon by eon, oxygen built up in our atmosphere. This was bad news for life on Earth because it had evolved in an oxygen-free world. To early Earth microbes, oxygen wasn't life giving. It was life threatening. Oxygen is very reactive, which means it latches onto other molecules very easily. Some oxygen reactions create toxins (poisons) that damage living cells. These toxins killed off most Earth microbes.

This tragedy had a bright side (as you may have guessed). A few microbes survived the disaster. They adapted to oxygen by making chemicals that protected them from oxygen's toxins. These microbes even found a way to use oxygen to get energy. Using oxygen gave the microbes a lot more energy—so much energy that complex animals (like humans) were able to evolve. We now call this way of getting energy "respiration."

Oxygen was important for another reason too. Oxygen in the atmosphere reacted to form ozone. Ozone blocks most UV radiation from the sun. Life was able to crawl out of the ocean and live on land. In the end, oxygen was a giant leap forward for life on Earth.

Today we all depend on oxygen—the gift of ancient microbes.

The green patches on these desert rocks are cyanobacteria.

Stories from the Rocks

Chris, Margarita, and their companions traveled to many rock art sites in the Sahara. Sometimes they visited rock art sites that their guide already knew about. Other times they went exploring across the sand. As they traveled, Chris and Margarita collected dirt and rock samples and looked for evidence of microbial life.

Chris found an outcrop of sandstone, the same kind of rock that shelters little forests of fungi and cyanobacteria in the Antarctic Dry Valleys. To Chris's surprise, this sandstone had no little green men hidden inside. Why not? Chris doesn't know; he hopes to return to this area to set up year-round sensors. He thinks that some spots in the Sahara, like some spots in the Atacama, may be too dry for life.

When the Land Rovers got stuck in the dunes, everyone got out and pushed.

There are sandstone cliffs in the Sahara.
The same kind of sandstone is found
in the Antarctic Dry Valleys.

Chris and Margarita also collected thin, light-colored rocks with smears of green on their undersides. The green smears are colonies of cyanobacteria. Each bacterium is impossibly small, but when enough crowd together, you can see them without a microscope. It's like gazing at a distant green mountain. You can't make out each tree, but you know you're looking at a forest.

Cyanobacteria have been on Earth for billions of years. Some are specially adapted to living in hot, dry places. Desert cyanobacteria are found in places such as California's Death Valley, South Africa's Kalahari, the less dry parts of Chile's Atacama, Israel's Negev Desert, and North Africa's Sahara. You might find desert cyanobacteria under rocks if you live in a hot, dry part of the American Southwest.

Like plants, cyanobacteria get energy from the sun. Enough sunlight can get through a thin, light-colored rock to reach cyanobacteria living

The travelers set up camp.

Margarita gathers a soil sample.

Ancient people left their handprints outlined on a rock.

on the underside. Living under a rock protects the cyanobacteria from the scorching heat of the desert sun. The shady undersides of rocks also trap moisture needed by the cyanobacteria.

Are desert cyanobacteria the same all over the globe? Or does each desert have a unique kind? To answer this question, Chris needs to gather as many rocks with cyanobacteria from as many deserts as possible. Chris collects many samples by himself or with students like Margarita. He also gets samples from other scientists. Lumpy packages arrive on his desk at NASA from all over the world.

All desert cyanobacteria look similar under a microscope. Chris will need genetic tests to figure out their differences. It could be they are all close kin carried by the wind to deserts all over the world. Or each desert may have unique cyanobacteria that live nowhere else.

"Maybe the same microbes settle everywhere, or maybe unique kinds evolve right where they are," said Chris. "You can extend the same logic to life in the universe. Could it spread between planets?"

New Clues in the Sahara

One day Chris, Margarita, and their companions visited a plateau near Karkur Talh, a valley known for its art. They visited a large rock overhang that once gave shelter to the long-lost people of the Sahara. Inside the shelter were pictures of hunters chasing lanky giraffes.

Behind Margarita are ancient carvings of people hunting giraffes.

Chris and Margarita's expedition discovered a rock art site.

Nearby they stumbled on a new site. On a curving rock wall, they discovered a painting of red and brown people with long necks, tiny heads, and ropes of white on their chests that might be necklaces or perhaps body paint.

The painting was just a small discovery, a tiny hint about life in the ancient Sahara. But little clues can add up to a lot.

Astrobiology uses a lot of little clues too. They come from the sandstone in the Dry Valleys, balloons over the Atacama, permafrost in Siberia, and rocks in the Sahara. Sometimes they come sealed under ice at the very bottom of the world.

The hot, dry Sahara has preserved this mummified goat. Could ancient life be preserved on cold, dry Mars?

Life Under Ice

Lake Hoare, Antarctica

A supply helicopter flies over icy Lake Hoare.

Can life survive beneath a thick, permanent cover of ice?

It's hard to imagine anything living at the bottom of a lake that's always covered by a thick slab of ice. Yet wherever there's liquid water, there may be life. In 1986 Chris went to Antarctica to look for life in the coldest, most isolated waters on Earth.

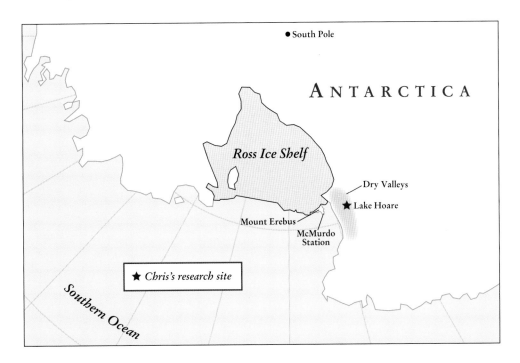

Scientists use sleds to haul equipment to the dive hole.

Chris uses the heating coil to melt through Lake Hoare's ice.

Gearing Up

Even during the Antarctic summer, Lake Hoare is completely frozen over. Its ice cover is sixteen feet (five meters) thick. To reach the lake's water, Chris and the other scientists laid a big metal heating coil on the

The hole is almost ready. When the ice is melted all the way through, the lake water will rise to fill the 16-feet-deep hole.

ice. They hooked the coil to a generator and waited. After thirty hours the coil melted a hole through the icecap and water rose to fill the hole. Time to suit up!

Chris didn't put on a swimsuit for his dive. He dressed in long underwear, a down vest, jeans, thick socks, gloves, and a woolen ski cap. Next Chris put a special dry suit on over his clothing. The dry suit was extra tall to fit all six feet six inches of him. The suit's bands fit snugly around Chris's neck, wrists, and ankles. Unlike a wet suit—the rubbery clothing divers and surfers wear to stay warm in cold water—a dry suit is designed to keep its wearer completely dry. A dry suit is warmer than a wet suit. That's a very good thing when you're diving in Antarctica.

Chris gets help with his flippers.

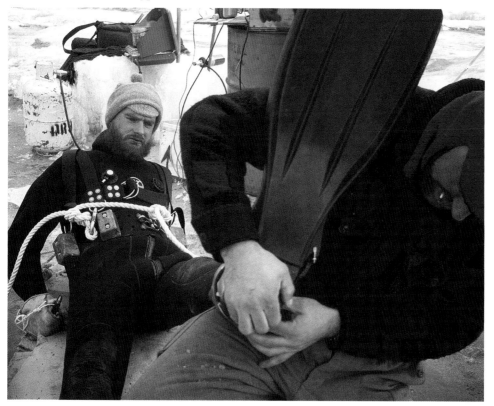

Green Guys at Work

Chris walked to the ice hole. He strapped on a tank, a regulator (to supply air from his tank), flippers, and weights. Then he put on his helmet. The helmet had a radio inside so that he could talk to the people helping him at the surface. Chris also had a rope tied around his waist to help him find his way back up to the hole—his only way out.

A dive hood and helmet go on last.

Chris gets ready to take the plunge.

After his helpers double-checked his equipment, Chris scooted to the edge of the hole and entered the water. Chris descended slowly to the bottom of the lake, a hundred feet down. It was surprisingly light under the ice cap. "Dim, but not dark. Enough light to read by," recalled Chris.

Even at the very bottom of an ice-covered lake at the very bottom of the world, life had taken hold. A greenish mat of microbes—algae—

Dense layers of microbes live
in extremely cold water at the
bottom of Lake Hoare.

covered the lake bed. Chris has a lot of respect for the gunky-looking stuff. "There's somebody green just about everywhere on Earth," Chris said later. "Green guys do all the work, and everybody else lives off them. Every ecosystem needs them."

Chris installed sensors at the bottom of the lake. The sensors recorded light levels and temperatures year-round. Like the microbes that lived nearby in the rocks of the Dry Valleys, the algae mats under Lake Hoare probably grew during the light-filled summer and slept through the long, dark Antarctic winter.

A diver collects samples of the microbes living on the bottom of Lake Hoare.

When Chris finished planting the sensors on the bottom, he swam toward the surface. The hole in the ice formed a bright halo overhead. When he reached the edge of the hole, Chris couldn't get out by himself because his equipment was heavy and awkward. The people waiting above helped drag him onto the ice. "Diving is actually pretty comfortable," said Chris later. "It's the people on the ice who shiver."

Chris remembered one dive when he was assisting scientist Dale Andersen. Dale was collecting algae samples from the bottom of Lake Hoare. A valve on Dale's tank began leaking and sending a rolling mass

Could a lake similar to this one (Lake Vanda in the Antarctic Dry Valleys) have existed on Mars?

of bubbles up into the dive hole. Alarmed, Chris radioed Dale to return to the surface. As Dale emerged from below, the high-pressure air shooting out of the tank sprayed water all over Chris. It froze instantly. "I looked like one big glazed donut," recalled Chris. "I dragged Dale out of the hole and waddled back to the hut to thaw out. Dale was nice and cozy in his dry suit!"

Alien Lakes, Alien Oceans

Chris studies Lake Hoare because it's the kind of lake that might have existed on Mars long ago. Even if Mars was never as warm as Earth,

This is an artist's conception of what an early Mars sea might have looked like.

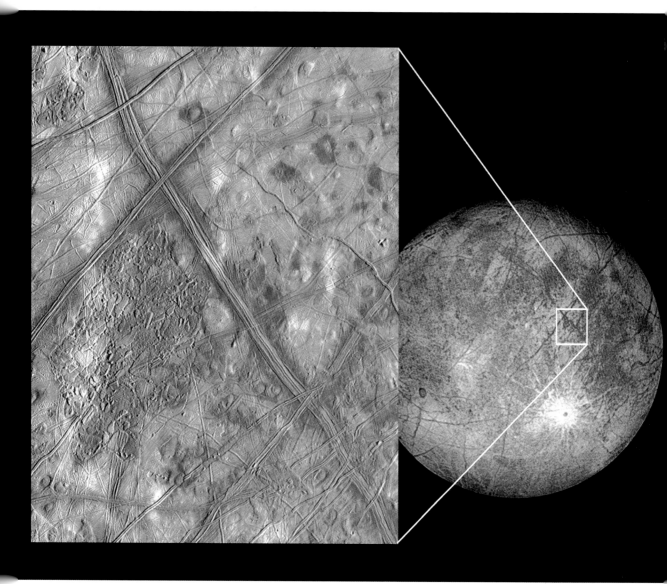

This close-up of Jupiter's moon, Europa, shows cracks in its icy surface.

it might have had ice lakes fed by melted snow. If "green things" can live under Antarctic ice, they might have lived in Martian lakes too. Chris hopes future Mars missions will be able to explore some Martian sites that may be dried-up lake beds. It would be a good place to look for evidence of lake-dwelling Martians.

Then there's Europa. Jupiter's moon has a thick ice cover, and there may be a salty ocean underneath. Europa's ice is probably miles thick; no light could reach the sea floor. But there are cracks in Europa's ice. Some water may get close enough to Europa's surface so that photosynthesis can occur. That's how green things on Earth make a living. There might also be hot-water vents at the bottom of Europa's ocean that could support life.

Someday scientists hope to send a special mission to Europa. A "cryobot" (ice robot) would use heat to melt its way through Europa's ice shell. When it reached water it would release a "hydrobot" (water robot). The hydrobot would explore Europa's dark, hidden ocean.

This is what a "hydrobot" might look like exploring Europa's ocean.

One thing is certain—our cryobots, hydrobots, rovers, landers, and astronauts will never run out of mysterious places to explore. Here on Earth, Chris and other astrobiologists will continue to search extreme environments for clues about what may be waiting for us.

Chris and the other scientists flew a pirate flag over their camp on Halloween. They didn't get any trick-or-treaters.

Conclusion
A Rose for the Red Planet

Chris checks an experiment near Death Valley, California.
He wants to find out how long it will take microbes to colonize
the undersides of the bottles.

In addition to his work in the world's most extreme environments, Chris
is helping NASA pick out landing sites for future Mars missions. In 2008
the *Phoenix Lander* will set down on Mars and use a robotic arm to dig
up a sample. It will check the sample for any chemicals that come from

living things. Another mission, the *Mars Science Laboratory*, will be a minivan-sized rover. It may go to the Red Planet as early as 2010. Chris is especially looking forward to *Mars Science Laboratory*. "The *Spirit* and *Opportunity* rovers were mobile, but dumb," says Chris. "All the science they did on Mars, I could do in one afternoon in a high school science lab. *Phoenix* will be smart, but immobile. *Mars Science Laboratory* will be both mobile and smart."

Someday NASA hopes to launch a Mars sample return mission that will bring Martian soils and rocks back to Earth for scientists to study. To astrobiologists, a Martian sample would be the most precious thing on Earth.

This is an artist's rendering of a rocket full of Mars samples blasting off to Earth.

The sun sets on Mars.

Chris hasn't forgotten his dream of sending astronauts to Mars. He thinks a first step would be to send a seed to Mars on a future mission. He wants to grow a flowering plant there, using Martian soil, sunlight, and nutrients. "There are two reasons to grow a plant on Mars," says Chris. "First of all, it's a cool thing to do. Second, if we send humans to Mars for any length of time, they will need to grow their own food. It would be a first step."

Not everybody thinks sending an Earth plant to Mars is a good idea. "Either people love it, or they are horrified," admits Chris. "But I think a flower blooming on Mars would be a wonderful thing."

Someday we may decide to take life with us to other planets. But many scientists, including Chris, think life is already out there somewhere. Of course, the universe is infinitely big. Alien life may be very small and difficult to find. It might be so strange that we will have a hard time recognizing it as life. We might not find it on Mars, Europa, or anywhere else in our solar system. But someday, when we point a telescope toward a distant point of light, we may find that Earth is not the only planet draped in blue and green.

This is an artist's rendering of a plant growing on Mars.

This is Mars's "Happy Face Crater" (Galle Crater).

This is a composite
of NASA images.

Researching Life on Earth—and Beyond

Believe it or not, this book began with an Internet search on frogs. I was looking for information on the wood frog, an amphibian that can survive Arctic temperatures. When I typed in "extreme environments," I found a huge amount of information not on frogs but on microbes. I learned about microbes that can survive without air, without light, and without anything we would think of as food; microbes that can survive extreme heat, cold, salinity, and acidity—even radiation; and microbes that can live again after sleeping millions of years.

Wow.

These extreme microbes led me to astrobiology. Astrobiology led me to Chris McKay. I drove to NASA and interviewed Chris for a children's science article. Our talk was so interesting that I decided I wanted to write a book.

Before writing a book I always start with careful research. Although the Internet is a handy place to begin, you should double-check any information you find online. Books and articles written by scientists or respected science writers are the most reliable sources. Before I began writing, I read a shelfful of books about Mars exploration, astronomy, astrobiology, and organisms in extreme environments. I read an eight-hundred-page college textbook on microbiology. I read scientific journals such as *Science* and *Nature* and scanned newspapers for science stories. I collected files of articles on the latest NASA missions and recent discoveries in astronomy and microbiology.

Author Pamela S. Turner and astrobiologist Chris McKay
discuss the book in Chris's NASA office.

Relatively well armed, I went back to Chris to learn more. He patiently described his field trips via computer images and photographs. He also showed me rock samples he's collected over the years. Finally, Chris and I took a field trip to check some of his sensor experiments in Death Valley. During the long car ride, we talked about his work and the future of astrobiology. You can learn a lot from books, but there's nothing like talking to a real expert to pull everything together.

When we returned from Death Valley, I gathered my files and books and started writing. Chris was kind enough to read my manuscript and make corrections. If any errors remain, however, the responsibility for them is entirely mine.

In doing my research I found resources that I think would be helpful if you would like to know more about astrobiology and space science. Turn the page and enjoy!

Scientists believe that the valleys in the Deuteronilus Mensae region on Mars may have been created by a flood of melted ice.

Resources

Further Reading

Breidahl, Harry. *Extraterrestrial Life: Life Beyond Earth?* (Life in Strange Places). Broomall, PA: Chelsea House, 2001.

———. *Extremophiles: Life in Extreme Environments* (Life in Strange Places). Broomall, PA: Chelsea House, 2001.

Grady, Monica. *Astrobiology.* Washington, DC: Smithsonian Institution Press, 2001.

Skurzynski, Gloria. *Are We Alone? Scientists Search for Life in Space.* Washington, DC: National Geographic Society, 2004.

Multimedia

Jenkins, Mark and Dale Andersen. *Life on Ice: Antarctica and Mars.* Carl Sagan Center, 2006. QuickTime movie, http://daleandersen.seti.org/

Butler, George. *Roving Mars.* IMAX movie. Burbank, CA: Walt Disney Pictures, 2006.

Internet Resources

Astrobiology Magazine
> **http://www.astrobio.net**
> Find news stories, discussions of hot topics, and image galleries on this NASA website.

The Astrobiology Web
> **http://www.astrobiology.com/**
> Read the latest astrobiology news from scientists all over the world.

Google Mars
> **www.google.com/mars/**
> Double-click and you're on Mars. You can choose a map color-coded by altitude, a black-and-white surface map, or an infrared map that shows temperature. The maps can take you to special features on Mars (mountains, craters, and canyons) and show you where spacecraft have landed.

NASA's Mars Exploration Program: Fun Zone
> **http://mars.jpl.nasa.gov/funzone_flash.html**
> Play games and download paper models on this website about NASA's Mars missions.

Mars Exploration Rover Mission
> **http://marsrovers.jpl.nasa.gov/home/index.html**
> Watch multimedia shows on the Mars rovers and view the images beamed back to Earth from Mars.

NASA Astrobiology Institute
> **http://nai.arc.nasa.gov/students/index.cfm**
> Read field reports from astrobiologists and analyze real data in the "For Students" section.

The Whole Mars Catalog
> **http://www.marstoday.com/**
> Look here for news and reference information on the Red Planet.

Of Special Interest to Educators

Mars Student Imaging Project
> **http://msip.asu.edu**
> Learn about a program that allows students to do real imaging work with scientists from NASA and Arizona State University.

NASA Astrobiology Institute
> **http://nai.arc.nasa.gov/**
> Dive into the "For Teachers" section for materials and classroom activities on the search for life beyond Earth.

NASA's Mars Exploration Program
> **http://mars.jpl.nasa.gov/classroom**
> Find workshops, resources, and educational programs on astrobiology and space science.

Roving Mars Movie
> **http://disney.go.com/disneypictures/rovingmars/**
> Click on "Educator's Guide" for a downloadable educator guide to the movie.

Acknowledgments

Science writers are always looking for great sources—respected scientists who have a knack for explaining complex subjects in a way anyone can understand. It's a bonus when the scientist is also a great guy. My deepest thanks go to Chris McKay for his patience, good humor, and willingness to share his experiences. It truly has been a pleasure.

My thanks also to those who generously shared their photographs or artwork: Dale Andersen, Corby Waste, Michael Donnellan, Kevin Hand, Margarita Maranova, Douglas Shrock, Jacek Wierzchos, and Andras Zboray.

At Charlesbridge I would like to thank my editor, Yolanda LeRoy. I had so much to say about astrobiology, but I was worried that my first draft was too long; Yolanda, bless her heart, asked me to write more. Her continuing guidance and encouragement are much appreciated. I am so very pleased with the "look of the book," and for that I'd like to thank Randi Rivers and Diane Earley for their hard work and artistry.

Finally, for their love, support, and tolerance of take-out foods, I would like to thank my husband, Rob, and my children, Travis, Kelsey, and Connor.

Photo Credits

Index

This photo of a Martian ridge
was taken by the *Spirit* rover.